Words By God's Grace

A Poetic Compilation About the Damage of Hurts and the Price of Choices

CHRISTINE GAIL GARCIA

Copyright Certificate of Registration

TXu 1-717-693 – 9/9/2010
- Take Me Instead
- The Valley

TXu 1-750-543 – 4/12/2011
- If You Only Knew
- Shelter My Family
- This Child (For Khloe)
- Which One Are You

TXu 1-776-388 – 9/21/2011
- The Potter's Hand
- The Road

TXu 1-793-900 – 2/1/2012
- Jesus' Walk
- My Service

TXu 1-815-394 – 6/16/2012
- Saying Goodbye
- The Tree Out My Window

TXu 1-877-639 – 6/28/2013
- Do Your Children Know You Love Them
- God's Eyes

- I Do – I Will
- I Wish
- I Wish I Could Have Known You
- Make Him Your Man
- Peace
- Sometimes
- Tranquility or Peace
- Words Unkind

TXu 1-996-669 – 8/21/2015
- Do We Trust God or Not
- Eternity Waits
- Highway To Heaven
- I'm Just a Sin Away
- No More Chances
- The Cost of Abortion Is Much Higher Than You Know

Txu 2-377-009 – 7/5/2023
- I Can't Run Away
- It
- Look To the Lord
- The Worst Day of Your Life or The Best Day of Their Life

For more information, email – cggarcia@christinegailgarcia.com

ISBN: 979-8-89316-931-7 (paperback)
ISBN: 979-8-89316-930-0 (eBook)

*To my husband, Andrew, who so unselfishly relinquished much of
"our time" to give me the quiet time to write and commune with God.*

*Without God's help, my poems would not be. His hands are all over
the pages of this book and not just in the places where I struggled
to find the right words or where the hurts became overwhelming.
These words flow through me, not from me. God is more than
an equal partner. He has been and is my guiding Light.*

CONTENTS

ACKNOWLEDGEMENTS

I'd like to acknowledge and thank the following people, each of whom played an important role in bringing this book to life:

Irene Garcia who not only read my book, but whose suggestions improved its quality immensely.

Eric Gonzales whose constant cheerleading and "My favorite author" greeting along with his prayers encouraged and kept me going.

Pastor Roger Tanner who sat with me and went over all the Bible verses in the book and helped with the selection and elimination process.

Dakota Reed who took the time to understand what I was trying to say and how I wanted to say it before recommending editing and proofreading changes.

Karen Pina, my mentor with the publishing company, who kept her sense of humor while guiding me, and without whose valuable knowledge and experience I would still be floundering.

FOREWORD

The *Words By God's Grace* books of poems deal mainly with my own life struggles. Within their pages, you will find pain and sorrow, tears of regret, and tears asking for forgiveness. But you will also find strength from belief in God and thankfulness and praise for who He is and what He has done for me. My journey hasn't always been easy or pleasant, mostly due to my own choices. But God has never left me nor given up on me.

As you journey with me through *Words By God's Grace*, and as the poems speak to you, you will be able to journal about your own life struggles. I hope that through this journey you will find strength and comfort from knowing there are other people who experience the same things, feel the same things, say the same things, do the same things, and have the same frustrations, and regrets.

But most importantly, I pray you never forget that the loving arms of our Savior, Jesus Christ, are just a prayer away and that through Him and by Him, our regrets can be turned into hope.

The Lord bless you, and keep you; The Lord make His face shine on you, And be gracious to you; The Lord lift up His countenance on you, And give you peace. (Numbers 6:24-26)

Do We Trust God or Not?

My problem is this yo-yo I carry around. I give a situation to God and then I take it back. All the blessings God has given me, and all the times He has guided and protected me I know; but I yo-yo anyway.

There are times I give an issue right back to God, but there are enough times where I lose sleep and peace worrying and trying to figure out a solution. Those are the times when, if I get any sleep at all, it's because I fall asleep from crying or exhaustion, or both.

Sooner or later, I give the situation back to God completely and get out of His way. Then I have peace again.

Just like Jacob in Genesis 32, we can react with worry, fear, and panic then go to prayer and then take the burden back again.

Cast thy burden upon the LORD, and he shall sustain thee: he shall never suffer the righteous to be moved. (Psalm 55:22)

Thou wilt keep him in perfect peace, whose mind is stayed on thee: because he trusteth in thee. (Isaiah 26:3)

Come unto me, all ye that labour and are heavy laden, and I will give you rest. (Matthew 11:28)

Be careful for nothing; but in every thing by prayer and supplication with thanksgiving let your requests be made known unto God. And the peace of God, which passeth all understanding, shall keep your hearts and minds through Christ Jesus. (Philippians 4:6-7)

Casting all your care upon him; for he careth for you. (1 Peter 5:7)

CHRISTINE GAIL GARCIA

Do We Trust God or Not?

Our faith must be strong, or peace will leave.
God's promises are true, and we must believe.
God will not forsake; He will not leave.
We are the ones who leave and then grieve.

When we take our concerns to God, we must leave them there.
But because answers don't always come right away,
we'll worry and stress and try to fix the mess.
What do we get for all our sweat? Gray
hairs, wrinkles, and no answers yet.

It all comes down to this: Do we trust God or not?
If we do, then this craziness we must stop.
What we gave God yesterday, we mustn't take back today.
God know what He's doing. Just trust and obey.

Stay in the Word. Remain in prayer.
Beware of doubt—Satan lives there.
Keep close to God; He'll see you through.
God's word is powerful, and His promises are true.

Written January 2013

CHRISTINE GAIL GARCIA

Do Your Children Know You Love Them?

After my mother died my dad was stationed in Japan, and I went to live with one of his sisters. I'm sure my aunt loved me, but all I remember of her are the spankings and being afraid. It was a different story with my uncle. I knew he loved me, and it's his love I remember.

I have prayed with women asking God to soften the hearts of their husbands, to help their husbands be more loving to their children, to be less harsh and distant. The hearts of these women are breaking because they see their husbands alienating their own children. The husbands don't know how to, can't, or won't show love, tenderness, and care for their children. These women see the damage done by their husbands that may never be repaired.

To my heartbreak, while my own sons loved their father and still do, the negative memories they have of their dad outweigh the positive ones. They know their dad worked hard to support his family, and that he was the first person anyone in the family called when they needed help. But if you ask my sons to describe their dad, the one phrase they will use is 'extremely uncomplimentary.'

Please don't let the memories your children carry with them of you be negative, bad memories. Leave them with memories of love and laughter. Raise them with godly, compassionate training in the way they should go.

And you, fathers, do not provoke your children to wrath, but bring them up in the training and admonition of the Lord. (Ephesians 6:4)

Fathers, do not exasperate your children, so that they will not lose heart. (Colossians 3:21)

Christine Gail Garcia

Do Your Children Know
You Love Them?

Do your children know you love them?
Can they see it in your face?
Do they hear it in your words and voice?
Do they cringe at your touch, or feel love in your embrace?

Take care how you deal with your children.
Keep anger and harshness away.
Check your actions and words with God first
before damage is done that stays.

Anger and harshness breed fear and hate.
I doubt you would love God if He treated you so.
God set the example; He showed the way.
For everyone's sake, it's best to obey.

Some children rebel. Some children hide.
Some children shut down and turn inside.
But all children are afraid of what you won't control.
And all children are hurt when love you don't show.

The scars can run deep. The pain can be great.
Love for you can be lost and replaced with hate.
Will you teach them to hate you? Will you drive them away?
Will you teach them to raise their children the very same way?

Be careful how you treat your children.
God placed them in your care.
He holds you accountable.
This sin I would not dare.

Written October 2012

CHRISTINE GAIL GARCIA

Eternity Waits

Eternity is coming. Maybe sooner than we think. It has been said that the best, safest, and surest way to prepare for eternity and guarantee that your residence will be in Heaven, is to live like every day is your last. That's all well and good. But if you haven't accepted Jesus Christ as your Lord and Savior; no amount of good works and living right will get you there. In fact, what awaits you is a living nightmare.

Revelation 19:19 – 21 describes the battle between Christ and His armies and the Beast, the Kings of the Earth, and their armies, and the end results. In verse 20 both the beast and the false prophet are seized and thrown alive into the lake of fire. Verse 21 says that **the rest** (their armies) **were killed.**

Revelation 20:12-15 describes the 2nd Resurrection (Resurrection to judgement for the dead).

Joel 3:1-2 and Matthew 25:31-46 deal with the Son of Man judging the nations in the Valley of Jehoshaphat (after the thousand-year reign). To those who refused to accept Christ and instead joined Satan, Jesus will say, "Depart from Me, you cursed, into the everlasting fire—And these will go away into everlasting punishment.

Penn Jillette posed the following questions to Christians regarding our belief in eternity and everlasting life in a YouTube video:

"If you believe that there is a Heaven and Hell, and people could be going to Hell or not getting eternal life .... how much do you have to hate somebody to believe that everlasting life is possible and not tell them?"

Here's the link to the video.

https://www.youtube.com/watch?v=6md638smQd8

We need to be prayer warriors for our unsaved family members and friends. We need to be positive examples for Christ and Christianity. We need to step out of our comfort zones and talk to our unsaved family members, friends, neighbors, and anyone God "puts in our path" (my husband calls it "the pitch") about Jesus and God.

CHRISTINE GAIL GARCIA

Eternity Waits

You say you're a good person, and I believe you are.
You try not to hurt people; you give to the poor.
But for you, there is no God.
There is this life and nothing more.

You believe this life we're living is the only chance we have.
And that when we die that's it, we're done, nothing left to tell.
You don't believe in Heaven. You don't believe in Hell.
Jesus lived, you will agree, but as a
mortal "man" like you and me.

You're right when you say this life we're living is the only
chance we have,
but not to live it to the fullest or to make our mark somehow.
Our lifetime is our only chance to choose which side we're on.
Jesus or Satan, Heaven or Hell. Eternity waits—choose well.

It doesn't matter how good you are, or
how much you help the poor.
What matters is the choice you make, which
side you're on, what stand you take.
Unbelief is a choice, a choice you are free to make.
But the consequences of such a choice
are too awful to contemplate.

Satan is happy to have you, no matter what you believe.
God will only take you if you submit to Him on your knees.
With Satan, you will burn and suffer misery untold,
but with Jesus as your Lord and Savior, eternity is gold.

Written February 2014

CHRISTINE GAIL GARCIA

God's Eyes

I know a young woman who thought she wasn't good looking and that she had no talent. She expressed these thoughts many times. The truth is, I could be talking about any number of other women or myself. No matter what I said I wanted to be, my stepmother always told me I wasn't smart enough, and I believed her. And like this young woman, I didn't think I was good looking either.

But as I watched, this young woman found love, married a wonderful man, and is now a wonderful, loving mother, raising her children.

I know another woman who has expressed these same feelings. She is one of the most gentle, caring, and loving women I know. She has the gift of making you feel so special and so loved.

Both these women know and love the Lord, and the Holy Spirit has blessed them both with gifts. Other women see their gifts and love them for how they use their gifts. But both these women, like many of us, listened to the world and to Satan and judged themselves by "man's" standards.

We need to remember and never forget that we are precious to God, that we are His children, and that He delights in us.

God created man in His own image, in the image of God He created him; male and female He created them. (Genesis 1:27)

Your hands fashioned and made me altogether, (Job 10:8a)

For You formed my inward parts; You wove me in my mother's womb. I will give thanks to You, for I am fearfully and wonderfully made; Wonderful are Your works, And my soul knows it very well. (Psalm 139:13-14)

Before I formed you in the womb I knew you; (Jeremiah 1:5a)

CHRISTINE GAIL GARCIA

God's Eyes

Why do we see ourselves as ugly when
in God's eyes we are beautiful?
Why do we call ourselves worthless when God calls us beloved?
Why do we keep condemning what God has already redeemed?
Why is it so hard for us to believe in what God sees?

Why do we look to man to determine our beauty?
Why do we look to man to determine our worth?
Why do we judge ourselves by the world's beliefs?
Why do we let man blind us to what God sees?

The world is ruled by Satan.
Man's vision is distorted by him.
Satan will condemn us cruelly.
Our insecurities he will use to win.

God's eyes are all that should matter.
Rebuke what the world has to say.
Find shelter in God, and trust in His word.
Satan's world can't tear you down that way.

Written July 2012

Highway To Heaven

Take a good look before you decide which road to take. One is narrow and one is wide. The narrow road looks restrictive, there are rules to be obeyed. The wide road has none; it seems we are totally free.

But take a closer look at the wide road. If you look hard you can almost see the end of the road and what you will see is people screaming, desperate to escape the fate that awaits them.

On the narrow road, on the other hand, people are running to the end, jumping, and shouting for joy at the fate that awaits them.

God gives us free will. We can choose to follow Him, or we can choose our own path and reject Him.

See, I have set before you today life and prosperity, and death and adversity; in that I command you today to love the Lord your God, to walk in His ways and to keep His commandments and His statutes and His judgments, that you may live and multiply, and that the Lord your God may bless you in the land where you are entering to possess it. But if your heart turns away and you will not obey, but are drawn away and worship other gods and serve them, I declare to you today that you shall surely perish. You will not prolong your days in the land where you are crossing the Jordan to enter and possess it. I call heaven and earth to witness against you today, that I have set before you life and death, the blessing and the curse. So choose life in order that you may live, you and your descendants, (Deuteronomy 30:15-19)

God won't force anyone to follow Him. He allows us to make up our own minds and to choose our own paths. Those who choose their own path and reject God will find that all paths except the one leading to God lead to Hell.

Enter through the narrow gate; for the gate is wide and the way is broad that leads to destruction, and there are many who enter through it. For the gate is small and the way is narrow that leads to life, and there are few who find it. (Matthew 7:13-14)

Hell was created for Satan and his angels. God never meant it for us. *Then He will also say to those on His left, 'Depart from Me, accursed ones, into the eternal fire which has been prepared for the devil and his angels; (Matthew 25:41)*

CHRISTINE GAIL GARCIA

Highway To Heaven

The road to damnation is as wide as can be.
Satan and the world will guide you for free.
The world is a tempter, all shiny and bright.
It's Satan's home and in it he delights.

Satan would have you love this world and its pleasures.
He knows it can keep you from God and the salvation He offers.
God says to leave this world. Satan asks why.
God says, "it will kill you." Satan says, "that's a lie."

On the highway to Heaven, the road is narrow, not wide.
It's the only way to salvation, and Jesus is the guide.
The more you value this world and the things that are in it,
the less willing you will be to choose this path of repentance.

When earth, and not Heaven, is what fills your soul,
the highway to Heaven will not be your goal.
You'll live for today with no thought of the hereafter.
You're practically handing your soul to Satan on a silver platter.

If you take the highway to Heaven, the world will lose its charm.
Your eyes will be open. Satan and his lies Jesus will disarm.
Your focus will change from earthly pleasures
to what awaits you in Heaven—salvation's treasures.

Each road has a cost, a price to be paid.
With Satan and the world, the price you will pay
is an eternity in Hell come judgment day.
With God, His Son paid the price—you just have to obey.

Written February 2015

I Can't Run Away

I don't like reading this poem. I don't like being reminded of that version of myself. Images and memories come flooding back, and I feel dirty all over again. No amount of scrubbing can make me feel clean or erase the past. I can't rewind my life and do things differently. Unlike fiction novels, TV shows, or movies, there is no time machine to use or door to walk back through.

I hate this poem, but the words speak the truth. The memories of sins we've committed can haunt all of us. I pay for my sins each time the memories return. I have been forgiven, I know that, and I am no longer that person.

As Pastor Jon Courson says, "Although there is forgiveness of sin, there are also repercussions; although God forgives and forgets, the scars remain." The images and memories I have of my sins will always be with me, and they aren't always dormant. And I have no control over when and how often they invade my waking hours.

be sure your sin will find you out (Numbers 32:23b)

"Can a man hide himself in hiding places So I do not see him?" declares the Lord. "Do I not fill the heavens and the earth?" declares the Lord. (Jeremiah 23:24)

But there is nothing covered up that will not be revealed, and hidden that will not be known. (Luke 12:2)

Do not be deceived, God is not mocked; for whatever a man sows, this he will also reap. 8 For the one who sows to his own flesh will from the flesh reap corruption, (Galatians 6:7-8a)

And there is no creature hidden from His sight, but all things are open and laid bare to the eyes of Him with whom we have to do. (Hebrews 4:13)

I Can't Run Away

I can't run away from the memories of my sins.
I can't get rid of them.
I can scrub and scrub until I'm red and raw,
but it does no good at all.

I stepped into the ring with Satan and sin,
and it left me battered and bruised.
I can't take back and I can't undo.
While it's true God forgives, we reap what we sow while we live.

Though I no longer play, I still must pay.
The memories haunt and torture my soul.
If not for God's mercy, if not for God's grace,
disease and death could have come my way.

I can't run away from the memories of my sins.
I can't get rid of them.
I can scrub and scrub till I'm red and raw,
but it does no good at all.

Written May 2016

CHRISTINE GAIL GARCIA

I Do - I Will

I wrote this for the wedding of my daughter and son-in-law, but it could be for anyone getting married. As I read the poem again, I think of my own marriage history—what I learned and what I hope my boys have learned.

I was divorced from my first husband and married for almost 27 years to my second husband when he passed away. I have been married since 2004 to my third husband.

Were all those years with my second husband wonderful, joyful, and smooth sailing? Of course not. Did we fight, scream, and holler at each other? Yes. Did we sleep as far away from each other as possible at times? Yep, many times. Did we hurt each other? Unfortunately, many times. Did we consider divorce, did we spend time apart? Yes, to both. Did it all work out? Yes, it did. Was it worth it? Yes, it was!

I learned a lot about what it takes to make a marriage work over the course of those years. I learned if you love, you forgive. I learned that compromise doesn't mean you lose. I learned that if it isn't life-threatening, it probably isn't worth arguing about or proving you're right. I learned that "I'm sorry" is a necessary part of the marriage vocabulary. I learned my "perfect" personality—my views, and ideas, what I said and how I said it—didn't always go over very well. I learned that even though I learned all of this, I can still have a hard time putting what I learned into practice.

There are times and seasons where marriage will be hard work. There are also times and seasons where marriage is wonderful and easy. Put God first and follow his guidelines and directions for marriage, and you will get through the tough times and seasons. You will grow together, and your love for each other and your marriage will be stronger. You will also have a powerful testimony of the benefits and joys of a Godly marriage.

Mark 10:9
Ephesians 4:2-3
Ephesians 5:21-33

Colossians 3:18-19
1 Corinthians 13:4-7
1 Peter 3:7; 4:8

CHRISTINE GAIL GARCIA

I Do - I Will

Today you have chosen to say *I will*.
For better or for worse, for richer or for poorer,
in sickness and in health, from this day forward.
Today you chose *til death do you part*. Today you chose *I will*.

This promise today, you make to each other.
This promise today, you make to God.
This promise isn't conditional. This promise doesn't depend.
It's a commitment you keep through thick and through thin.

The choice to stay you will make every day.
Some days this choice will be easy.
Some days this choice may be hard.
But choose to stay you must if God you obey.

God doesn't say you can leave when it gets tough.
God doesn't say you can walk away.
These vows are meant for a lifetime.
God says if you chose His way, you must stay.

If you love God and you love His Son,
if you put them first, then victory you have won.
When God is the head, your marriage will thrive,
for God's way you will always seek and strive.

Written November 2012

CHRISTINE GAIL GARCIA

I Wish

"There are only two kinds of people in the end: everlasting splendours (those who say to God, "Thy will be done.") or immortal horrors (those to whom God says, in the end, "Thy will be done."). All that are in Hell, choose it. Without that self-choice, there could be no Hell." — C.S. Lewis, *The Great Divorce*

God won't force anyone to follow Him. He allows us to make up our own mind and to choose our own path.

"You have never talked to a mere mortal…. But it is immortals whom we joke with, work with, marry, snub, and exploit— immortal horrors or everlasting splendors." — C.S. Lewis, *The Weight of Glory*

People have a choice. Talk to them. Talk to them about the choices. Explain to them the rewards or consequences of these choices.

Therefore I said to you that you will die in your sins; for unless you believe that I am He, you will die in your sins. (John 8:24)

Jesus said to him, "I am the way, and the truth, and the life; no one comes to the Father but through Me. (John 14:6)

And there is salvation in no one else; for there is no other name under heaven that has been given among men by which we must be saved. (Acts 4:12)

But a natural man does not accept the things of the Spirit of God, for they are foolishness to him; and he cannot understand them, because they are spiritually appraised. (1 Corinthians 2:14)

For the wisdom of this world is foolishness before God. For it is written, "He is the one who catches the wise in their craftiness"; (1 Corinthians 3:19)

Therefore, to one who knows the right thing to do and does not do it, to him it is sin. (James 4:17)

For all that is in the world, the lust of the flesh and the lust of the eyes and the boastful pride of life, is not from the Father, but is from the world. (1 John 2:16)

I Wish

I wish you could feel what I feel.
I wish you had the gift that I have.
I wish you could experience God in your life.
I wish I could explain so that you would believe.

I wish your eyes could see.
I wish your ears could hear.
I wish your heart would believe
what your mind can't conceive.

Do you doubt like Thomas what you cannot see?
Do you really think this world is giving you all you need?
Do you think God is cruel because of the world you see?
Have you turned from what you once believed?

Are your lifestyle choices getting in the way?
Do you honestly believe this life is all there is?
Can you not see where your beliefs are wrong indeed?
Do you think you're a good person and that's all you need?

How can I get through to you? What can I say?
How can I help you see the errors of your way?
I can show you God's Word. It's powerful indeed.
I can pray that the Holy Spirit your heart will receive.

Written September 2012

CHRISTINE GAIL GARCIA

I Wish I Could Have Known You

I had an abortion. This poem and one other poem in this book deal with this issue. Both poems were extremely hard to write. I avoided working on this book for a long time after writing these two poems because of how difficult the page for each poem was going to be.

Abortion isn't mentioned in the Bible. But scripture clearly states that God creates and forms us in the womb, and that He knows us from the time of conception. Exodus 21:22-23a details the punishment for causing a woman to lose or miscarry her unborn child. This is proof that God considers an unborn child a person, and that life is created at the moment of conception.

If men struggle with each other and strike a woman with child so that she gives birth prematurely, yet there is no injury, he shall surely be fined as the woman's husband may demand of him, and he shall pay as the judges decide. But if there is any further injury, then you shall appoint as a penalty life for life, (Exodus 21:22-23a)

You shall not murder. (Exodus 20:13)

For You formed my inward parts; You wove me in my mother's womb. I will give thanks to You, for I am fearfully and wonderfully made; Wonderful are Your works, And my soul knows it very well. My frame was not hidden from You, When I was made in secret, And skillfully wrought in the depths of the earth; Your eyes have seen my unformed substance; And in Your book were all written The days that were ordained for me, When as yet there was not one of them. (Psalm 139:13-16)

There are six things which the Lord hates, Yes, seven which are an abomination to Him: Haughty eyes, a lying tongue, And hands that shed innocent blood, (Proverbs 6:1617)

Because I gave my life to Christ many years ago, I know Heaven is my final home. With this knowledge comes the realization that I will see my child again. I began to wonder what our meeting would be like, what the child might say to me. I both dread and look forward to that meeting.

CHRISTINE GAIL GARCIA

I Wish I Could Have Known You

I wish I had a name. I wish I had, had a chance.
But you gave me no name. You gave me no chance.
I guess you didn't want me to happen. You didn't want me to be,
because almost as soon as it began, you took my life from me.

Would I have been so much trouble?
Couldn't a way have been found?
I guess it was easier to get rid of me
than to try to work it out.

Have you ever thought about me?
Have you ever shed a tear?
Have you ever thought of all we missed?
Or was I just a burden you didn't want to bear?

So much lost, so much missed.
My first words, my first steps,
love and laughter, hugs and kisses,
hopes and dreams, birthdays and Christmas.

I wish I could have known you.
I wish I could have lived.
I don't understand the choice you made.
I wish you would have chosen life for me instead.

Written March 2013

CHRISTINE GAIL GARCIA

If You Only Knew

There was a time when I looked at the women in my church and felt very unworthy next to them. I felt that their worse sins were not nearly as bad as mine. I felt like I was wearing a mask. I was afraid that if they knew the sins of my youth—even though they knew the "me" now—they would look at me differently.

But God sent an angel to me at a retreat—the speaker. I was able to talk and pray privately with her. I left the retreat at peace with both my past and present self.

I thank God every day for His saving grace, and I want people to know that if God can forgive me, He can forgive anyone.

He has not dealt with us according to our sins, Nor rewarded us according to our iniquities. For as high as the heavens are above the earth, So great is His lovingkindness toward those who fear Him. As far as the east is from the west, So far has He removed our transgressions from us. Just as a father has compassion on his children, So the Lord has compassion on those who fear Him. For He Himself knows our frame; He is mindful that we are but dust. (Psalm 103:10-14)

All that the Father gives Me will come to Me, and the one who comes to Me I will certainly not cast out. (John 6:37)

that if you confess with your mouth Jesus as Lord, and believe in your heart that God raised Him from the dead, you will be saved; (Romans 10:9)

for "Whoever will call on the name of the Lord will be saved." (Romans 10:13)

CHRISTINE GAIL GARCIA

If You Only Knew

If you only knew the person that I was.
If you only knew the things that I have done.
If you only knew, if you only knew.
You would say "no way would God forgive me."
You would say "no way would He wash my sins away.
No way, no way would God save me."

If I stood before you, no mercy would I see.
No forgiveness, no grace would be given to me.
I would stand forever a liar, a cheat, a thief.

Where would you stand if judged by me?
Would you stand forever a liar, a cheat, a thief?
Judgment and justice, or mercy and grace.
The choice is yours, your decision to make.

Take the advice of a sinner—a liar, a cheat, a thief.
Take the advice of a sinner who chose mercy and grace.
Run, don't walk to the Mercy seat.
Get down on your knees; give yourself to the Lord.
Run, don't walk; throw yourself at His feet.

If you only knew the joy and relief.
If you only knew what God so freely gives.
If you only knew. If you only knew.
I wouldn't need to say "run, don't walk, to the Mercy seat.
Get down on your knees, give yourself to the Lord.
Run, don't walk; throw yourself at His feet."

Written May 2011

CHRISTINE GAIL GARCIA

I'm Just a Sin Away

There are times when I get close to sinning, but then I'm able to stop myself because I go to God. But a lot of the time I end up stepping in and having to work my way out. Usually, it's my attitude. I get judgmental or critical, don't want to do something, don't want to give of my resources, or get mad at God over what I feel is wrongly happening to me. There have also been times when it has taken me a long time to forgive someone.

How do I get away from Satan's grip? I go to God and His word. I pray for help and forgiveness. I remember what God has done for me. I'm a sinner and I will always be a sinner, but I'm a sinner saved by grace. I love the Lord and I refuse to let Satan win. I refuse to give Satan bragging rights.

For if you forgive others for their transgressions, your heavenly Father will also forgive you. But if you do not forgive others, then your Father will not forgive your transgressions. (Matthew 6:14-15)

Do not judge so that you will not be judged. For in the way you judge, you will be judged; and by your standard of measure, it will be measured to you. Why do you look at the speck that is in your brother's eye, but do not notice the log that is in your own eye? (Matthew 7:1-3)

"Do not judge, and you will not be judged; and do not condemn, and you will not be condemned; pardon, and you will be pardoned. Give, and it will be given to you. They will pour into your lap a good measure—pressed down, shaken together, and running over. For by your standard of measure it will be measured to you in return." (Luke 6:37-38)

So, as those who have been chosen of God, holy and beloved, put on a heart of compassion, kindness, humility, gentleness and patience; bearing with one another, and forgiving each other, whoever has a complaint against anyone; just as the Lord forgave you, so also should you. Beyond all these things put on love, which is the perfect bond of unity. (Colossians 3:12-14)

Christine Gail Garcia

I'm Just a Sin Away

I'm just a sin away, only a sin away—
a sin away from falling, a sin away from losing all.
It's a constant battle with my nature, the natural state of man.
Because Adam and Eve ate the apple, sinful is what I am.

I could go the way of Cain
and let anger and jealousy take hold of my soul.
I could plot evil and revenge
and cut myself off from God's blessings that flow.

I could go the way of Korah
and let desire and envy take over and control.
I could rebel against God's will for me
and find that although I breathe, I am dead in my soul.

I could go the way of Balaam
and for personal gain and reward,
seek to circumvent the will of God
and bring the threat of death upon me from the Lord.

Then there is Ananias and Sapphira who both lied and died.
And don't forget the Israelites themselves.
All the times they disobeyed the Lord
and all the times they cried.

But I have a weapon that is strong and true.
The word of God will see me through.
It's all I need and nothing more
to keep from falling through Satan's door.

Written August 2015

CHRISTINE GAIL GARCIA

It

I hate "its." I don't know anybody who likes them. "Its" will come to some of us more than others, but we will all deal with "its." "Its" will change us, one way or another. That change is up to us.

People who have a close, personal relationship with God before an "it" happens manage an "it" with peace and comfort, knowing that God will get them through. God doesn't promise to always deliver us from "its." What He does promise is to be with us and get us through. They may not understand, but because of their relationship with God, they know they can trust Him.

People who don't have a strong, personal relationship with God don't know they can trust Him. They don't understand His promises and they don't know God's character. Many times, all they see and believe is that God is cruel.

The time to develop a close, personal relationship with God is before an "it" happens. Jumping ship and abandoning God comes from a lack of trust, and a lack of trust comes from not knowing God. There is more at stake than just having to deal with an "it." The decision to abandon God has eternal consequences.

Trust in the Lord with all your heart And do not lean on your own understanding. In all your ways acknowledge Him, And He will make your paths straight. (Proverbs 3:5-6)

The steadfast of mind You will keep in perfect peace, Because he trusts in You. (Isaiah 26:3)

These things I have spoken to you, so that in Me you may have peace. In the world you have tribulation, but take courage; I have overcome the world. (John 16:33)

Be anxious for nothing, but in everything by prayer and supplication with thanksgiving let your requests be made known to God. And the peace of God, which surpasses all comprehension, will guard your hearts and your minds in Christ Jesus. (Philippians 4:6-7)

CHRISTINE GAIL GARCIA

It

"It" has happened. "It" has hit.
Here we are, dealing with "it."
What do we do? How will we be?
What will "it" reveal about the strength of our belief?

Will we rejoice in the Lord?
Will we trust Him each day?
Will we give in to fear?
Will we walk away?

Fear can overwhelm so that we cannot see.
And when tears flow so freely, to be angry is easy.
Rejoicing can be tough in the midst of an "it."
And hearts can close to God's fellowship.

"Its" can be difficult to swallow. "Its" can be hard to take.
That God allows "its" must be a mistake.
Why does God do it? How can it be?
How many will walk away from God because they cannot see?

"Its" help us to grow in our walk with the Lord.
Through "its" we learn to trust Him more and more.
"Its" can show us the error of our ways
and return us to God from our wandering days.

Written March 2016

CHRISTINE GAIL GARCIA

Jesus' Walk

We were blessed by God to be able to go to Israel. At the end of the second day, I was struck by the fact that I didn't feel Jesus. After all, I was walking where Jesus had walked, even on the same stones sometimes. I was disappointed and felt like I was missing out. My husband said he felt the same way.

That night, God set me straight. He woke me up out of a sound sleep and told me it wasn't about walking in the places where Jesus had walked. It was about walking *how* Jesus walked and the relationship we have with Him. Visiting Israel was about making the Bible come alive when I read it. My relationship, and thereby my walk, with God isn't determined by where I am physically. It's determined by where I am spiritually.

My son, if you will receive my words And treasure my commandments within you, Make your ear attentive to wisdom, Incline your heart to understanding; For if you cry for discernment, Lift your voice for understanding; If you seek her as silver And search for her as for hidden treasures; Then you will discern the fear of the Lord And discover the knowledge of God. (Proverbs 2:1-5)

You will seek Me and find Me when you search for Me with all your heart. (Jeremiah 29:13)

But I say, walk by the Spirit, and you will not carry out the desire of the flesh. (Galatians 5:16)

If we live by the Spirit, let us also walk by the Spirit. (Galatians 5:25)

CHRISTINE GAIL GARCIA

Jesus' Walk

I have walked in Galilee, where Jesus taught and walked.
I have walked the streets of Jerusalem,
where Jesus bled and died.
I have stood on stones He walked upon
and seen the same sunrise.
I have walked where Jesus walked, but
do I walk how Jesus walked?

Do I walk how Jesus walked, or walk to a different beat?
Do I walk how Jesus walked, or does another guide my feet?
Do I look to His example or ignore His path each day?
Do I follow in His footsteps or travel a different way?

It's not about where Jesus walked.
It's not about where Jesus taught.
To say I have walked where Jesus walked
carries little weight with Him.
To walk how Jesus walked is what will save me from my sin.

Written November 2011

CHRISTINE GAIL GARCIA

Look to the Lord

Have you ever felt like you blew it so badly that God has turned His back on you? Do you believe your life is so messed up that God won't want anything to do with you?

When we make mistakes, we beat ourselves up longer and harder than anybody else. I should know. I've had plenty of practice. We also give up on ourselves and condemn ourselves to continue living a life without God.

But all it takes is a humble heart, an outstretched hand, and calling on God—and He's right there. And guess what! Once you ask Him in, He's there to stay.

But from there you will seek the Lord your God, and you will find Him if you search for Him with all your heart and all your soul. (Deuteronomy 4:29)

If you seek Him, He will let you find Him; (1 Chronicles 28:9c)

You will seek Me and find Me when you search for Me with all your heart. (Jeremiah 29:13)

But as for me, I will watch expectantly for the Lord; I will wait for the God of my salvation. My God will hear me. (Micah 7:7)

So I say to you, ask, and it will be given to you; seek, and you will find; knock, and it will be opened to you. For everyone who asks, receives; and he who seeks, finds; and to him who knocks, it will be opened. (Luke 11:9-10)

For the Son of Man has come to seek and to save that which was lost. (Luke 19:10)

CHRISTINE GAIL GARCIA

Look to the Lord

When your troubles are so many you see no way out,
when you feel lost and burdened beyond despair,
when your sins feel so heavy your heart is broken,
turn to the Lord and go to Him in prayer.

If you feel like you've gone too far and lost your way,
if you think it's too late and there's no turning back,
if you don't believe that God would ever want you,
take a look at Calvary and the sinner saved that day.

No one who seeks is too far from God's reach.
No one who seeks is left wandering astray.
Comfort and peace are free for the taking.
Call on God's name and your sins are washed away.

Look to the Lord, don't be afraid.
Look to the Lord, and your life He will save.
Cling to His Son, the rock of salvation.
Cling to the Lord—let His Word guide your way.

Written July 2011

CHRISTINE GAIL GARCIA

Make Him Your Man

When a husband treats his wife selfishly, harshly, or unkindly, it can damage more than just the marriage—it can damage the wife. When a husband berates his wife, hollering and cussing at her whenever he doesn't get what he wants, another tear is created in the fabric of their relationship.

The Bible is very clear on how a husband is supposed to treat his wife. It also clearly says that what comes out of the mouth is from the heart. The fruits of a husband are seen in how he treats and talks to his wife and his children.

He who finds a wife finds a good thing And obtains favor from the Lord. (Proverbs 18:22)

Her children rise up and bless her; Her husband also, and he praises her, saying: (Proverbs 31:28)

For the mouth speaks out of that which fills the heart. (Matthew 12:34b)

It is not what enters into the mouth that defiles the man, but what proceeds out of the mouth, this defiles the man. (Matthew 15:11)

But the fruit of the Spirit is love, joy, peace, patience, kindness, goodness, faithfulness, gentleness, self-control; against such things there is no law. (Galatians 5:22-23)

So husbands ought also to love their own wives as their own bodies. He who loves his own wife loves himself; for no one ever hated his own flesh, but nourishes and cherishes it, just as Christ also does the church, (Ephesians 5:28-29)

Husbands, love your wives and do not be embittered against them. (Colossians 3:19)

CHRISTINE GAIL GARCIA

Make Him Your Man

How long must she suffer?
How much more can she endure?
She's hanging on by a thread.
How many more tears must she shed?

Is his heart toward You hardened?
Is it completely beyond repair?
Is he totally owned by Satan?
Is there no hope through prayer?

She says that she is broken.
She's not who she used to be.
So much hurt he has inflicted,
this husband of hers, you see.

Your timing, I know, is perfect.
But it worries me what I see.
A husband and a father
causing his wife such misery.

He says he knows the Bible.
He says he has read Your word.
But I see no fruits of the Spirit,
and I fear You may never be heard.

Please don't give up on him.
Please don't let Satan win.
I know You want his salvation.
Please, Lord, make him Your man within.

Written August 2012

CHRISTINE GAIL GARCIA

My Service

If you're like me, there has been a time when God has allowed someone in your life that you must care for. And if you're like me, that person was difficult to deal with, caused you grief, and/ or broke your heart. When this happens, it isn't always about the other person. It could be about you. God could be using the person to work in you. This doesn't mean that you can't or won't be a testimony of God's love to the other person. In fact, if you allow God to work in you, your actions will plant the seeds of God's love. It's all in how you deal with the situation.

When I try to deal on my own, without seeking God, I can only take so much before I start feeling trapped with no way out. I wallow in self-pity and anger. But then I talk to God, confess my sin, seek forgiveness, and ask for strength. You see, I don't do it just for the other person, and I don't do it to make myself look good. I do it for the glory of God. And when I seek God, He gives me strength and He replenishes my strength.

Whatever you do, do your work heartily, as for the Lord rather than for men, knowing that from the Lord you will receive the reward of the inheritance. It is the Lord Christ whom you serve. (Colossians 3:23-24)

whoever serves is to do so as one who is serving by the strength which God supplies; so that in all things God may be glorified through Jesus Christ, to whom belongs the glory and dominion forever and ever. Amen. (1 Peter 4:11b,c)

CHRISTINE GAIL GARCIA

My Service

When I'm tired of doing,
when I'm feeling abused,
when my thoughts turn hateful,
and the other I accuse—

Satan will feed,
and the flames He will fan.
Satan will work
to keep me just as I am.

When the other is selfish,
when the other is mean,
when the other is difficult,
and no thought for me is seen—

It's easy to get angry.
It's easy to get upset.
It's easy to have an attitude
and to say and do things I will later regret.

But who am I serving, the person or God?
Will my service bear fruit that speaks of the Lord?
If I do for the person, I will never succeed.
If I do for the Lord, His strength I receive.

This service is mine, its burden to bear.
The Lord has not lifted but, keeps me here.
This battle, I know, is best fought on my knees
where God's comfort and strength I will receive.

Written December 2011

CHRISTINE GAIL GARCIA

No More Chances

Each day we live is an opportunity to choose Jesus and eternal life. There will be no more chances once we take our last breath.

And inasmuch as it is appointed for men to die once and after this comes judgment, (Hebrews 9:27)

These will go away into eternal punishment, but the righteous into eternal life. (Matthew 25:46)

But for the cowardly and unbelieving and abominable and murderers and immoral persons and sorcerers and idolaters and all liars, their part will be in the lake that burns with fire and brimstone, which is the second death. (Revelation 21:8)

People must choose to accept or reject God. Those who have chosen to reject God will suffer eternally in the Lake of Fire. Those who choose God will spend eternity in Heaven.

And he causes all, the small and the great, and the rich and the poor, and the free men and the slaves, to be given a mark on their right hand or on their forehead, and he provides that no one will be able to buy or to sell, except the one who has the mark, either the name of the beast or the number of his name.

(Revelation 13:16-17)

Then another angel, a third one, followed them, saying with a loud voice, "If anyone worships the beast and his image, and receives a mark on his forehead or on his hand, he also will drink of the wine of the wrath of God, which is mixed in full strength in the cup of His anger; and he will be tormented with fire and brimstone in the presence of the holy angels and in the presence of the Lamb. And the smoke of their torment goes up forever and ever; they have no rest day and night, those who worship the beast and his image, and whoever receives the mark of his name." (Revelation 14:9-11)

God doesn't want anyone to suffer for eternity.

who desires all men to be saved and to come to the knowledge of the truth. (1 Timothy 2:4)

The Lord is not slow about His promise, as some count slowness, but is patient toward you, not wishing for any to perish but for all to come to repentance. (2 Peter 3:9)

CHRISTINE GAIL GARCIA

No More Chances

We lie, we cheat, we steal.
We are selfish, self-centered, thoughtless, and cruel.
We abuse and torture, murder and rape.
We indulge our fleshly desires; we fornicate.

We ignore the homeless, the suffering, the weak.
We strive to eliminate other cultures and beliefs.
We rewrite the Bible to suit our needs,
or we call it fiction and refuse to believe.

Some say, "I'm a good person, what more do I need?
That's my ticket. I know I will succeed."
Some refuse to believe Jesus is the only way.
"There are many ways to Heaven," they will shrug and say.

Some say that what matters is the work you do.
Some say all that matters is if God has chosen you.
Some don't believe in life after death.
Salvation, Heaven, and Hell are to them, just a myth.

What will it take for each of us to believe?
What will it take for us to get down on our knees?
A day is coming when it will be too late.
A day is coming when we will have sealed our fate.

No more chances to heed the call.
No more chances to change our fate.
No more chances to pass through Heaven's gate—
Condemned to burn for eternity is what awaits.

Written August 2015

CHRISTINE GAIL GARCIA

Peace

All worry does is rob of us peace. Worry doesn't solve any problems. Talking things over with God and giving our problems to Him brings immediate peace. At least, it does for me. Even if the problems aren't solved by the end of our time together, I'm at peace.

There are times when nothing seems to be going right, when it seems like as soon as one trial ends another begins, when there are so many prayer requests for our family and others that we could spend all day on our knees. Whether our prayer requests are for one huge problem or many small ones, we have to give them to God and trust that He will handle them. If we don't totally and completely trust God to take care of our issue(s), peace won't come.

Cast your burden upon the Lord and He will sustain you; He will never allow the righteous to be shaken. (Psalm 55:22)

Trust in the Lord with all your heart And do not lean on your own understanding. In all your ways acknowledge Him, And He will make your paths straight. (Proverbs 3:5-6)

Peace I leave with you; My peace I give to you; not as the world gives do I give to you. Do not let your heart be troubled, nor let it be fearful. (John 14:27)

These things I have spoken to you, so that in Me you may have peace. (John 16:33a)

Be anxious for nothing, but in everything by prayer and supplication with thanksgiving let your requests be made known to God. And the peace of God, which surpasses all comprehension, will guard your hearts and your minds in Christ Jesus. (Philippians 4:6-7)

casting all your anxiety on Him, because He cares for you. (1 Peter 5:7)

Peace

When we go every day and talk to the Lord,
when we give Him our problems
and trust how He solves them,
the peace we receive is a blessed reward.

When we look to ourselves and lean not on the Lord,
when we hold on to our problems
and trust not in God to solve them,
a lack of peace is our only reward.

Just like the Ark of old, God will steer us true.
And just like the Israelites, God will get us through.
But we have to trust, we have to believe
totally and completely in what may be hard to conceive.

Don't turn to the left or to the right.
Follow the path that the Lord has set.
Walk by faith and not by sight.
Don't miss what God wants to do in your life.

If peace and joy are what you seek,
if happiness and contentment you value indeed,
put your walk with God at the top of your list,
and let the Lord take care of the rest.

Written March 2013

CHRISTINE GAIL GARCIA

Saying Goodbye

The hurt, pain, and sorrow of losing a loved one can feel unbearable. For Christians, this grief is made bearable if we know that our loved one is with the Lord. We know the joy and peace they are experiencing, and we know goodbye is not permanent.

The real pain and heartache comes when a loved one who doesn't know the Lord dies. Then we know goodbye is final and forever. When we aren't sure if our loved one knew the Lord, it can be just as painful.

Never let a chance pass by to talk to those you care about, about the forgiveness, grace, mercy, and love of our Lord and Savior Jesus Christ. To have to wonder and not know if you will see them again is a terrible thing to have to endure.

When I wrote this poem, my daughter-in-law had recently lost her grandmother. My husband and I had the privilege of taking communion with her and her family not long before her grandmother passed away. What a joy it was to watch Nana sing, pray, and praise the Lord. Death held no fear for her. She knew where she was going, and she knew who she would be seeing.

At the funeral there was grieving, but there was also rejoicing because they knew that this crusader for Christ was now in the presence of her Lord.

He who believes in the Son has eternal life; but he who does not obey the Son will not see life, but the wrath of God abides on him. (John 3:36)

For the wages of sin is death, but the free gift of God is eternal life in Christ Jesus our Lord. (Romans 6:23)

And the testimony is this, that God has given us eternal life, and this life is in His Son. He who has the Son has the life; he who does not have the Son of God does not have the life. (1John 5:11-12)

Saying Goodbye

The circle of life is both joyous and cruel.
A new life begins and another life ends.
We rejoice at a birth; we mourn at a death.
This should be reversed because of man's sins.

We are born into this world filled with sin,
and here we must dwell until this life ends.
Those who walk with the Lord know to this world they don't
belong–
and when this life ends, they know God has called them home.

The time to pray for a loved one is before their life ends.
Pray that their heart isn't hardened, and that Satan doesn't win.
Pray that they have asked God to dwell within,
and pray forgiveness for all their sins.

If you know your loved one walked with the Lord,
let your heart rejoice, for they go to their reward.
Angels have escorted them through the pearly gates
and God has taken them into His embrace.

If you walk with the Lord, you will see them again.
For when you leave this world, you will join them in Heaven.
So, grieve for your loss and feel your pain.
Say your goodbyes, but don't let sorrow reign.

Written May 2012

CHRISTINE GAIL GARCIA

Shelter My Family, Lord

Everyone wants to protect their family members from hurtful words and unkind actions. When family members are made to feel like they aren't good enough and that they are just tolerated, it hurts.

This poem was my prayer to God to keep my sons from being hurt too much and from hurting in return.

Cast your burden upon the Lord and He will sustain you; He will never allow the righteous to be shaken. (Psalm 55:22)

He who dwells in the shelter of the Most High Will abide in the shadow of the Almighty. (Psalm 91:1)

For you have made the Lord, my refuge, Even the Most High, your dwelling place. No evil will befall you, Nor will any plague come near your tent. For He will give His angels charge concerning you, To guard you in all your ways. (Psalm 91:9-11)

Deliver me, O Lord, from my enemies;]I take refuge in You. (Psalm 143:9)

Do not say, "I will repay evil"; Wait for the Lord, and He will save you. (Proverbs 20:22)

But I say to you, love your enemies and pray for those who persecute you, so that you may be sons of your Father who is in heaven; for He causes His sun to rise on the evil and the good, and sends rain on the righteous and the unrighteous. (Matthew 5:44-45)

Pursue peace with all men, and the sanctification without which no one will see the Lord. See to it that no one comes short of the grace of God; that no root of bitterness springing up causes trouble, and by it many be defiled;

(Hebrews 12:14-15)

CHRISTINE GAIL GARCIA

Shelter My Family, Lord

Shelter my family, Lord.
Be unto us as You were to David.
Silence those whose hearts are hardened toward us.
Stop the tongues that speak two ways.

Cover our ears when evil is spoken.
Close our mouths so we return not evil for evil.
Let our hearts not be hardened against those who abuse us.
Let the arrows not pierce and damage our souls.

Your way is forgiveness.
Help us to forgive those whose hearts are turned against us.
Your way is love. Help us to love when no love is given.
Strengthen us, Lord. Help us to always walk in Your way.

Written April 2011

CHRISTINE GAIL GARCIA

Sometimes

Every day, as Christians we make conscious and deliberate choices to sin or not to sin. Satan is constantly trying to seduce us by tempting us with the things of the world. And if left to its own, our sinful nature—which is on the side of Satan—would be our downfall.

Battling with my sinful nature is something I must do daily. Sometimes I am strong, and sometimes I am weak. When I'm strong, I don't feel the presence of Satan at all. When I'm weak, I can feel him hovering over me, waiting for me to fall. When I'm strong, I'm standing on the solid rock of Jesus. When I'm weak, I'm standing on the cliff with one foot hanging over the edge.

This battle isn't one I can win on my own. The only way I can win this battle is to put on the whole armor of God, spend time daily with Him, and stay in His Word.

Put on the whole armour of God, that ye may be able to stand against the wiles of the devil. For we wrestle not against flesh and blood, but against principalities, against powers, against the rulers of the darkness of this world, against spiritual wickedness in high places. *Wherefore take unto you the whole armour of God, that ye may be able to withstand in the evil day, and having done all, to stand. Stand therefore, having your loins girt about with truth, and having on the breastplate of righteousness; And your feet shod with the preparation of the gospel of peace; Above all, taking the shield of faith, wherewith ye shall be able to quench all the fiery darts of the wicked. And take the helmet of salvation, and the sword of the Spirit, which is the word of God: Praying always with all prayer and supplication in the Spirit, and watching thereunto with all perseverance and supplication for all saints; (Ephesians 6:11-18)*

Submit yourselves therefore to God. Resist the devil, and he will flee from you. (James 4:7)

Be sober, be vigilant; because your adversary the devil, as a roaring lion, walketh about, seeking whom he may devour: (1 Peter 5:8)

CHRISTINE GAIL GARCIA

Sometimes

Sometimes I feel like I'm on the edge of a cliff
with one foot hanging over the edge.
Sometimes I feel like I'm safe and sound
with both feet firmly on the ground.

Sometimes I feel the breath of the devil.
Sometimes I don't feel his presence at all.
Sometimes I feel so close to falling.
Sometimes I feel no danger at all.

Sometimes I feel the devil waiting,
expecting my stumble and fall.
I hear all the negatives he whispers in my ear.
The fight to ignore him I'm losing; is clear.

When I know my next step will be over the edge
and my soul is in turmoil and I have no rest,
I run for cover; I run to the cross.
I cling to God's promises. They stand the test.

God promises to love, provide, and protect.
His arms are my fortress. His love is my rock.
God's word is my sword, armor, and shield.
Against God, the devil has no power; He must yield.

Written December 2012

CHRISTINE GAIL GARCIA

Take Me Instead

I wrote this poem for non-believers. I wanted to write a poem non-believers could relate to when it came to what God and Jesus did for them. So, I prayed and asked God for help.

God reminded me of my feelings as my husband lay dying. Stroking my husband's head and kissing his brow, I would have given anything to take his place.

God also reminded me of how I felt when the doctor told me my son had less than two years to live without a transplant. I would have given any organ to my son, and I would have given anything to take his place.

I know I'm not alone in how I feel. Every parent or spouse can relate to the loss of either a child or a spouse, even if they have never experienced it. I bet we would all say, "Take me instead."

Just as the Son of Man did not come to be served, but to serve, and to give His life a ransom for many (Matthew 20:28; Mark 10:45)

For God so loved the world, that He gave His only begotten Son, that whoever believes in Him shall not perish, but have eternal life. For God did not send the Son into the world to judge the world, but that the world might be saved through Him. He who believes in Him is not judged; he who does not believe has been judged already, because he has not believed in the name of the only begotten Son of God. (John3:16-18)

Christ redeemed us from the curse of the Law, having become a curse for us—for it is written, "Cursed is everyone who hangs on a tree"— (Galatians 3:13)

For there is one God, and one mediator also between God and men, the man Christ Jesus, who gave Himself as a ransom for all, the testimony given at the proper time. (1 Timothy 2:5-6)

Christ, who through the eternal Spirit offered Himself without blemish to God (Hebrews 9:14b)

CHRISTINE GAIL GARCIA

Take Me Instead

A child is dying. A mother is crying and
through her tears she says,
"I'd gladly give my life for hers. Please, take me instead."

There is no hope. A father's heart is broke
and through his tears he says,
"I'd gladly give my life for his. Please, take me instead."

A wife is dying. A husband is cry-
ing and through his tears he says,
"I'd gladly give my life for hers. Please, take me instead."

She strokes his head. There is no hope. Kisses his brow, this
man she loves,
and through her tears she says, "Please, take me instead."

All can understand the pain. All can understand the love.
A parent for a child, a husband, and a wife.
There would be no thinking twice, the offer a genuine sacrifice.
From somewhere deep inside our soul:
take me instead, take me instead.

There is no hope. God's heart is broke.
Condemned by sin, His people will die.
But then the Son steps forth and through His tears God hears
"I'll gladly give my life for them. Take me instead.
I understand the sacrifice. I'll willingly pay the price."

God sent His Son to die in our place.
Would you give your child, your husband, or wife?
Would you pay the price, make the sacrifice?
How deep is your love? How much deeper is His?

What will you do with this gift you've been given?
Will you let it be in vain, this sacrifice, or
welcome the Lord God and his Son,
Jesus Christ, into your life?

Written June 2011

CHRISTINE GAIL GARCIA

The Cost of Abortion
Is Much Higher Than You Know

I wish I didn't have to write this poem or this page. For years, an abortion was just something I'd had, just another matter-of-fact part of my life. But God wasn't going to let it stay that way. He started small: a jab here, a jab there, slowly increasing the pressure and frequency of the jabs until I had to face the truth.

I had to admit what an abortion was and what I had done. I will never forget that I killed my own child and that I killed a child of God. And each time I read the two poems dealing with this, I'm broken all over again.

Healing has come because God loved me enough to bring me to brokenness and repentance. Forgiveness has come because God loved me enough to sacrifice His Son, Jesus Christ, for my sins.

If men struggle with each other and strike a woman with child so that she gives birth prematurely, yet there is no injury, he shall surely be fined as the woman's husband may demand of him, and he shall pay as the judges decide. But if there is any further injury, then you shall appoint as a penalty life for life,

(Exodus 21:22-23)

Did not He who made me in the womb make him, And the same one fashion us in the womb? (Job 31:15)

Your hands made me and fashioned me; (Psalm 119:73a)

For You formed my inward parts; You wove me in my mother's womb. I will give thanks to You, for I am fearfully and wonderfully made; Wonderful are Your works, And my soul knows it very well. (Psalm 139:13-14)

Thus says the Lord who made you And formed you from the womb (Isaiah 44:2a)

Thus says the Lord, your Redeemer, and the one who formed you from the womb, (Isaiah 44:24a)

Before I formed you in the womb I knew you, (Jeremiah 1:5a)

CHRISTINE GAIL GARCIA

The Cost of Abortion
Is Much Higher Than You Know

I know my baby is in Heaven, even though
I killed her here on earth.
I want so much to see her, but will she want to see me?
Will she resemble her dad or me, or maybe
someone else in the family tree?
Will she be all grown up, or a baby still be?

Too long it has taken me to say I'm sorry.
Too long she has waited to hear those words from me.
Is she crying for joy that the words have been said,
while I'm crying in pain over the deed that I did?

I thought I couldn't keep her.
I knew I wouldn't be able to let her go.
I thought she would plunge me into poverty,
and I didn't want my son to suffer so.

Babies weren't even formed yet, or so we were told.
There was nothing to kill, just fluids to go.
But you cannot be pregnant with just fluids alone.
And the cost of abortion is much higher than you know.

The screams of a baby ripped from its mother's womb are silent
to our ears,
but they bring the whole of Heaven to tears.
A life torn to shreds and potential forever lost.
My God, how can a baby be so easy to toss?

Written March 2014

The Potter's Hands

The idea for this poem came from one of my pastor's sermons. So many people think that they can't come to God until they "clean up" their lives and stop doing the "bad" things. But God wants us to come to Him just as we are. Once we give ourselves to Him, the work really begins. As long as we will let Him, God will keep working in us. His whole purpose and desire is to see us become more and more like Him.

Behold, I have refined you, but not as silver; I have tested you in the furnace of affliction. (Isaiah 48:10)

But now, O Lord, You are our Father, We are the clay, and You our potter; And all of us are the work of Your hand. (Isaiah 64:8)

"Can I not, O house of Israel, deal with you as this potter does?" declares the Lord. "Behold, like the clay in the potter's hand, so are you in My hand, O house of Israel. (Jeremiah 18:6)

CHRISTINE GAIL GARCIA

The Potter's Hands

The Potter's hands are gentle.
The Potter's hands are strong.
His wheel is always turning,
the shaping never done.
He works to mold us in His image:
Father, Spirit, Son.

Clay that is worthless,
clay that is marred,
in the hands of the Potter
will become priceless,
will be restored.

His pots are meant for Heaven.
His blood purchased our clay.
But He can't start if we don't accept Him,
and He can't finish if we don't stay.

With pressure He shapes us.
With fire He strengthens us.
He works through our lives,
our problems and trials.
His will, not ours; His glory be done.
We are shaped to His image:
Father, Spirit, Son.

Written April 2011

The Road

How many times have I prayed to God to forgive me for the same past sins? There are too many times to count. God has already forgiven and forgotten them. Why do I keep condemning myself? Why don't I let go and move on? I don't because I am ashamed. Because I know the "me" that stands before Jesus and God. I know the "me" that is asking for salvation, asking to be forgiven, and asking for a place in Heaven. And I know that I don't deserve any of it.

Satan's sneaky and wily. He knows the exact buttons to push for each of us, and he'll try them all in his attempt to pull us away from God, including making us feel unworthy. On our own, we can't stand against Satan, but the Word of God gives us the tools we need to be victorious against Satan's attacks.

Therefore there is now no condemnation for those who are in Christ Jesus. (Romans 8:1)

Finally, be strong in the Lord and in the strength of His might. Put on the full armor of God, so that you will be able to stand firm against the schemes of the devil. For our struggle is not against flesh and blood, but against the rulers, against the powers, against the world forces of this darkness, against the spiritual forces of wickedness in the heavenly places. Therefore, take up the full armor of God, so that you will be able to resist in the evil day, and having done everything, to stand firm. Stand firm therefore, having girded your loins with truth, and having put on the breastplate of righteousness, and having shod your feet with the preparation of the gospel of peace; in addition to all, taking up the shield of faith with which you will be able to extinguish all the flaming arrows of the evil one. And take the helmet of salvation, and the sword of the Spirit, which is the word of God. (Ephesians 6:10-17)

Submit therefore to God. Resist the devil and he will flee from you. (James 4:7)

If we confess our sins, He is faithful and righteous to forgive us our sins and to cleanse us from all unrighteousness. (1 John 1:9)

You are from God, little children, and have overcome them; because greater is He who is in you than he who is in the world. (1 John 4:4)

CHRISTINE GAIL GARCIA

The Road

Why do we keep looking back at the road behind us?
On the road behind, we were lost and wandering astray.
The devil waits there to invade our
minds and condemn our souls.
He tells us we are not worthy while all our sins he displays.

The road ahead shines brightly with the glory of God.
On it we can see Calvary, where Jesus
fought and died for you and me.
"The victory is mine,'" Jesus says. "The devil has no hold on you.
As my lamb, you're white as snow—my blood
cleansed your sins from head to toe."

Why do we keep condemning ourselves?
Why do we keep replaying our sins?
Why do we let the devil attack us so? Why do we listen to him?
Jesus doesn't remember our sins. We got
on our knees; we asked Him in.

Whenever the road behind begins to haunt us,
whenever the devil tries to invade and condemn,
claim the blood of Jesus, put on the armor of God.
Call on the name of the Lord. The devil
cannot stand against Him.

Written May 2011

CHRISTINE GAIL GARCIA

The Tree Out My Window

I was watching this tree one day when it was really rainy and windy; and I marveled at the fact that in all the years this tree has been standing, the wind hasn't been able to break the one really bent branch off or blow the entire tree down. If the branch was growing straight up, it would probably be the tallest branch on the tree.

I realized that while the wind could bend the branches, it couldn't uproot the tree because obviously the tree had very strong, deep roots.

From that thought, my mind jumped to how I am like the tree—and how, because I cling to the Lord, I can weather any storm.

How blessed is the man who does not walk in the counsel of the wicked, Nor stand in the path of sinners, Nor sit in the seat of scoffers! But his delight is in the law of the Lord, And in His law he meditates day and night. He will be like a tree firmly planted by streams of water, Which yields its fruit in its season And its leaf does not wither; And in whatever he does, he prospers. (Psalm 1:1-3)

The Lord is my strength and my shield; My heart trusts in Him, and I am helped; Therefore my heart exults, And with my song I shall thank Him. The Lord is their strength, And He is a saving defense to His anointed. Save Your people and bless Your inheritance; Be their shepherd also, and carry them forever. (Psalm 28:7-9)

When the whirlwind passes, the wicked is no more, But the righteous has an everlasting foundation. (Proverbs 10:25)

CHRISTINE GAIL GARCIA

The Tree Out My Window

It has branches bent from the force of the wind.
Its leaves are tossed all about.
But while some branches are bent, the tree does not break.
It must be firmly rooted in the ground.

I watch that tree stand against the wind.
Even though some branches bend low,
it does not give; it does not break.
It must be holding on to something great.

Like the tree out my window, I am bent and scared.
Life has left its mark on me.
My heart has ached; my mind has despaired.
My body has faltered and tired.

To see the tree standing after all it has endured
is a constant reminder to me
that while I may bend, I will not break
if I am holding on to something great.

The tree is a picture for all who will see
of what God does for those who believe.
No matter your troubles, no matter how great.
if you cling to the Lord, you may bend—but not break.

Written March 2012

CHRISTINE GAIL GARCIA

The Valley

I started this poem in high school. I wasn't going to include it in this book because I didn't feel it belonged. However, after listening to prayer requests and praying for them, I knew this poem belonged in the book.

Once I graduated from high school, I was able to leave home and escape a living situation that left scars for a long time. I returned a year later for a visit, and all the memories and pain came flooding back over me. This poem addresses all those feelings.

Parents, we are to love our children. God doesn't tell us not to discipline our children, but He does warn against discipline without love and about discipline fueled by anger.

Parents, we can destroy or severely damage our relationship with our children by what we say and do to them. I know. My relationship with my father and stepmother was ruined, and the love my boys have for their father was damaged by their relationship with him too.

Fathers, do not provoke your children to anger, but bring them up in the discipline and instruction of the Lord. (Ephesians 6:4)

Fathers, do not exasperate your children, so that they will not lose heart. (Colossians 3:21)

The Valley

Up on a mountain far away, I view this place unsure.
Afraid to enter, I remember too clearly the pain of living there.
It cannot hide its real self from me; not even a mask will do.
I know too well what lies within and I
fear it through and through.

I feel its heat even way up here; its sky is so unsure.
It's hell down in that valley, though it looks like Eden from here.
I escaped and I'm free, but love draws me
back with a pain too great to bear.
I'm all twisted up for I love, hate, and
fear all that lies down there.

I shouldn't have come; it's torture for me,
but love doesn't die in a year.
I remember the wrongs, but also the rights,
and these memories release my tears.

"Oh God! What happened to my valley?"
I ask each night in my prayers.
That valley below once meant home and all that it holds dear.
Now it's just a place where I lived for a time,
filled with memories of love, hate, and fear.

Written 1969

CHRISTINE GAIL GARCIA

The Worst Day of Your Life
OR The Best Day of Their Life

I have a dear friend who, in two-and-a-half years, lost all three of her children – first her son, then her daughters. As we were visiting one afternoon, we began talking about how her grandchildren were doing. As expected, they were each dealing with the loss of their mother in their own way. My friend told me how her youngest grandson told her that the day his mother died was and would always be the worst day of his life. I asked her what her response was. My friend told me that she told her grandson that the day could either be the worst day of his life, or the best day of his mom's life.

My stepchildren lost their mother one New Year's Eve. Now they have a tough time with New Year's Eve every year. When I wrote this poem, I was thinking about my friend, but also about the four of them.

As Christians, while the loss of a loved one brings hurt and pain, we can find comfort in the knowledge that if they belonged to the Lord, we know where they are and that we aren't saying goodbye but see you later.

Precious in the sight of the Lord Is the death of His godly ones. (Psalm 116:15)

He who believes in the Son has eternal life; but he who does not obey the Son will not see life, but the wrath of God abides on him. (John 3:36)

For the wages of sin is death, but the free gift of God is eternal life in Christ Jesus our Lord. (Romans 6:23)

And the testimony is this, that God has given us eternal life, and this life is in His Son. He who has the Son has the life; he who does not have the Son of God does not have the life. (1John 5:11-12)

CHRISTINE GAIL GARCIA

The Worst Day of Your Life
Or The Best Day of Their Life

Someone you love is gone, never to return.
Never to see their face, never to hear their voice.
No more laughter, no more time together.
This date of each year, it's been ruined forever.

A hole so deep, it can never be filled.
A hurt so strong, it can never be healed.
A heart overwhelmed by the ache and the pain.
A mind so numb that it can't explain.

The worst day of your life, you'll never forget.
It's seared in your memory; it's branded on your heart.
Each year the day brings fresh heartache to bear,
remembering the one you lost and hold dear.

You can let the date be the worst day of your life,
but if the one whom you lost belonged to the Lord,
celebrate the date from this day forth.
Take your eyes off your hurt and look to where they are.

Written September 2021

CHRISTINE GAIL GARCIA

This Child (For Khloe)

I wrote this poem for my granddaughter's dedication before she had open-heart surgery at seven-and-a-half months.

It's been over ten years since I wrote this poem and the precious baby girl, now becoming a young lady, has changed her father and has made him a better man in so many ways. I'm so proud of him and so grateful for the journey this precious baby—and now young lady—has taken him on.

Behold, children are a gift of the Lord, The fruit of the womb is a reward. (Psalm 127:3)

And whoever receives one such child in My name receives Me; but whoever causes one of these little ones who believe in Me to stumble, it would be better for him to have a heavy millstone hung around his neck, and to be drowned in the depth of the sea. (Matthew 18:5-6)

See that you do not despise one of these little ones, for I say to you that their angels in heaven continually see the face of My Father who is in heaven. (Matthew 18:10)

But Jesus said, "Let the children alone, and do not hinder them from coming to Me; for the kingdom of heaven belongs to such as these." (Matthew 19:14)

CHRISTINE GAIL GARCIA

This Child (For Khloe)

This child is precious to you.
This child is precious to God.
Children are a gift from God,
but they still belong to Him.
Be careful what you do with God's gift.

Do not withhold them from God.
Do not withhold God from them.
Teach them God's ways.
Remember: by example you lead.
The path you set them on is the path
they will follow all their days.

Be careful how you treat God's gift.
Through the eyes of this child, God looks at you.
What does He see?
Through the ears of this child, God hears you.
What does He hear?
Through the heart of this child, the laughter and joy,
God feels the depth of your love.
What does He feel?

Remember that while this child is precious to you,
this child is more precious to God.
Never forget that children are a gift from God,
but they still belong to Him.
Be careful what you do with God's gift.

Written March 2021

CHRISTINE GAIL GARCIA

Tranquility or Peace

(In memory of Michelle)

This poem has taken on an even stronger message for me after watching our twenty-two-year-old granddaughter's courage and strength during her five-month battle in the hospital. She endured so much suffering and pain. She never complained, she never gave up, and her faith in God never wavered. In the beginning, she told Grandpa and me that she was ready to go home, whether it was her home on earth or her home in Heaven. I had to leave the room to cry. Michelle's battle ended on December 22, 2016, when she went home to God.

I didn't want any of it to happen. I wanted our nice, quiet, happy life. I wanted Michelle. Grandpa wanted to keep hearing Michelle say, "I love you, Grandpa." We didn't want this struggle. We didn't want this storm. You don't bury your grandchildren. They bury you.

In the blink of an eye, tranquility can be gone. Mine has disappeared too many times in my life. I don't know how people go through storms in their life if they don't have God. The only thing that gets me through the storms is God – His peace, His comfort, His strength.

The Lord is near to the brokenhearted And saves those who are crushed in spirit. (Psalm 34:18a)

The steadfast of mind You will keep in perfect peace, Because he trusts in You. (Isaiah 26:3)

The Lord is good, A stronghold in the day of trouble, And He knows those who take refuge in Him. (Nahum 1:7)

Peace I leave with you; My peace I give to you; not as the world gives do I give to you. Do not let your heart be troubled, nor let it be fearful. (John 14:27)

These things I have spoken to you, so that in Me you may have peace. In the world you have tribulation, but take courage; I have overcome the world. (John 16:33)

Blessed be the God and Father of our Lord Jesus Christ, the Father of mercies and God of all comfort, who comforts us in all our affliction (2 Corinthians 1:3-4a)

CHRISTINE GAIL GARCIA

Tranquility or Peace

Tranquility or peace:
which one will it be?
Which one do I pray for?
Which one do I need?

Do I pray for tranquility,
for a smooth sailing life
with no bumps in the road
and no struggles or strife?

Do I pray for God's peace
no matter life's struggles or strife,
when the road is a mess
and there's no smooth sailing in sight?

Tranquility is fine
but it goes in a flash
whenever the devil
launches an attack.

Tranquility only comes
when my life is carefree.
God's peace, on the other hand,
is constant and strong for all to see.

God's peace is there, no matter my life.
God's peace calms my heart, no matter my strife.
God's peace calms the storm raging within.
God's peace is there because I give the battles to Him.

Tranquility or peace:
which one will it be?
There's only one answer.
I pray for God's peace.

Written August 2012

CHRISTINE GAIL GARCIA

Which One Are You?

I have known people who are like what I describe in this poem. I have known atheists who are more than willing to have you pray for them when they are going through difficult and troubled times but will deny God's existence the rest of the time. I have known people who worship God when everything is going great but turn from God when times get tough. And I have had the pleasure of knowing and watching Christians who praise and worship God in both good and troubled times.

With God, there is no playing at being Christian. Either you are or you aren't. You can't have it both ways.

"Because I called and you refused, I stretched out my hand and no one paid attention; And you neglected all my counsel And did not want my reproof; I will also laugh at your calamity; I will mock when your dread comes, When your dread comes like a storm And your calamity comes like a whirlwind, When distress and anguish come upon you. "Then they will call on me, but I will not answer; They will seek me diligently but they will not find me, Because they hated knowledge And did not choose the fear of the Lord. "They would not accept my counsel, They spurned all my reproof. "So they shall eat of the fruit of their own way And be satiated with their own devices. "For the waywardness of the naive will kill them, And the complacency of fools will destroy them. "But he who listens to me shall live securely And will be at ease from the dread of evil." (Proverbs 1:24-33)

No one can serve two masters; for either he will hate the one and love the other, or he will be devoted to one and despise the other. You cannot serve God and wealth. (Matthew 6:24)

And without faith it is impossible to please Him, for he who comes to God must believe that He is and that He is a rewarder of those who seek Him. (Hebrews 11:6)

So because you are lukewarm, and neither hot nor cold, I will spit you out of My mouth. (Revelation 3:16)

CHRISTINE GAIL GARCIA

Which One Are You?

You remember God when you are in trouble.
You remember God when you are in pain.
You remember God when times are tough.
It is then that you call on His name.

But when life is good and going smooth, you forget about God.
When life is good and going smooth,
you don't remember His name.
And when life is good and going smooth, you claim the fame.
It is then that you think you don't need His name.

Or are you a fair-weather friend?
God is good, God is great when life is good, and life is great.
But when life brings storms and is filled with
pain, is God the one you blame?
And do you curse His Holy name?

Or do you raise your hands and sing praises to His name?
Do you give God glory in sunshine and in rain?
Do you kneel always at God's throne, humbled by His grace?
Do you walk with God and always seek His face?

Which one are you? Which one are you?

Written July 2011

Words Unkind

I've said them. I'm sure a lot of people have, especially with family. We know the buttons to push, the words to say when we want to strike out and hurt. Unkind words aren't reserved just for family, though; friends and strangers are also the recipients of unkind words. Isn't it funny, though, how we think differently when the words are coming *from* us versus when they are directed *at* us?

In relationships, unkind words can build a wall between two people or destroy the bridge between them. With each hurtful word, the wall gets higher, or the gap in the bridge gets wider. Before you know it, you can't climb over the wall or bridge the gap at all.

That old saying, "Sticks and stones may break my bones, but words will never hurt me" isn't true. Words hurt and they can hurt for a long time. What has been said can never be taken back.

Do not let your speech cause you to sin (Ecclesiastes 5:6a)

Keep your tongue from evil And your lips from speaking deceit. (Psalm 34:13)

Death and life are in the power of the tongue, (Proverbs 18:21a)

He who guards his mouth and his tongue, Guards his soul from troubles. (Proverbs 21:23)

For the mouth speaks out of that which fills the heart. (Matthew 12:34b) see also (Luke 6:45b)

It is not what enters into the mouth that defiles the man, but what proceeds out of the mouth, this defiles the man. (Matthew 15:11)

But the things that proceed out of the mouth come from the heart, and those defile the man. (Matthew 15:18)

Let no unwholesome word proceed from your mouth, (Ephesians 4:29a)

Words Unkind

Why do we say words unkind?
Why must we tear another down?
What is it that compels us to speak?
What is it that we need or seek?

Is jealousy the reason for these words we speak?
Is our own hurt so great it can breed only hate?
Are we self-absorbed with no thought for the other?
Are we building ourselves up at the expense of another?

We pay a price for words unkind.
We harden our hearts; we harden our minds.
We damage or destroy more relationships than we know.
We obviously forget that we reap what we sow.

Of all the commandments, the greatest is love.
And we grieve the Father, we grieve the Son
when the words that we speak, the things that we say
hurt another and push love away.

The Holy Spirit has no room to dwell
in a heart without love and cannot stay.
And God's presence in our lives will begin to fade
as the Holy Spirit is pushed away.

Written April 2013

CHRISTINE GAIL GARCIA

Stay Connected

Thank you for reading *A poetic compilation about the damage of hurts and the price of choices,* my new book in the Words By God's Grace series.

Visit my website and join my email list—two free handouts await you.

https://christinegailgarcia.com/

Follow me on

YouTube
https://www.youtube.com/@ChristineGailGarcia

Facebook
https://www.facebook.com/wordsbygodsgrace

My grandmother was a Titanic survivor.
Check out my page for her.
Maud Sincock Roberts Titanic survivor
https://www.facebook.com/christinegail.garcia.7/

Amazon author page
https://www.amazon.com/author/christinegailgarcia

Or email me
cggarcia@christinegailgarcia.com

Thank you for spending time with me. I hope our time together has blessed, encouraged, and strengthened you. If this book has blessed you in any way, I would be very grateful if you would take the time to write a review on Amazon and/or Goodreads.